Who eats who in City Habitats?

Robert Snedden

FRANKLIN WATTS
LONDON • SYDNEY

Designer: Cali Roberts
Editor: Constance Novis
Art Director: Peter Scoulding
Editor-in-Chief: John C. Miles
Picture Research: Diana Morris
Artwork: Ian Thompson

© 2005 Franklin Watts

First published in 2005
by Franklin Watts
96 Leonard Street
London
EC2A 4XD

Franklin Watts Australia
Level 17/207 Kent Street,
Sydney
NSW 2000

ISBN 0 7496 6082 1

Dewey classification number: 577.5'6

A CIP catalogue record for this book is
available from the British Library.

Printed in Malaysia

PICTURE CREDITS

Deborah Allen/Still Pictures: 9
Joe Blossom/OSF: 15
Kent Breck/Animals Animals/OSF: 12
Jim Corwin/OSF: 20
Foto Natura/FLPA: 8
Jamie Harron/Ecoscene: 26
Nick Hawkes/Ecoscene: 10
M. Timothy O'Keefe/Alamy: 17
Mike Lane/NHPA: 23
Wayne Lawler/Ecoscene: 13
Michael Maconachie/Ecoscene: 18
Benny Odeur/Still Pictures: 4
OSF: 7
Ray Pfortner/Still Pictures: 27
Robert Pickett/Ecoscene: 22
Jochen Tack/Still Pictures: 6
Alan Towse/Ecoscene: 21
A & J Visage/Still Pictures: 14
Carl Vomberger/Still Pictures: 16
Ian West/OSF: 5
Ken Wilson/Ecoscene: 19
Konrad Wothe/OSF: front cover, 1, 25

*Every attempt has been made to clear copyright.
Should there be any inadvertent omission please apply to
the publisher for rectification.*

Note to parents and teachers
Every effort has been made by the Publishers to ensure
that the websites in this book are suitable for children,
that they are of the highest educational value, and that
they contain no inappropriate or offensive material.
However, because of the nature of the Internet, it is
impossible to guarantee that the contents of these sites
will not be altered. We strongly advise that Internet
access is supervised by a responsible adult.

Contents

Food and energy

Rodents quickly learned that humans were a good source of food.

All living things share certain basic needs. One of these is the need for a place to live. The place where a living thing makes its home is called its habitat. For some, this is the rainforest, for others, deserts or mountains.

Living in towns and cities

For many of us, our habitat – the place where most of us make our homes – is in a town or city. Other living things have also adapted to life in towns and cities. They pass through as visitors or stay and live there as permanent residents. In towns and cities, they find everything they need to survive, especially supplies of food.

Yummy!

In a city like New York there may be ten times as many rats as people – all of them munching on our food!

The chain begins

All organisms need energy to survive. They get this from their food. Plants can make their own food by capturing energy from sunlight through photosynthesis (see page 7).

Unlike plants, animals can't make their own food, so they have to find a food supply within their habitat. For many animals this means eating plants. By doing so they take a share of the energy that the plants captured from the sun.

Other animals eat the plant-eaters. This forms a food chain, such as the one on the right. At each link in the chain energy is passed along from one living thing to another.

Who Eats Who?

plant material (seeds)

mouse

cat

Feeding squirrels are a common sight in cities.

The newest habitat

Towns and cities are the youngest of all the world's habitats. Rainforests, for example, may be millions of years old, but people only started to build homes for themselves a mere 12,000 or so years ago when they began to settle in one place as farmers.

To animals, settlements mean food. As settlements grew into towns and cities more and more animals made their homes there. They found food in the rubbish and scraps in the city parks and gardens.

First link

Where do the food chains begin in city habitats? Just as in any other habitat, the chains start with plants.

The difference is that whereas the plants in a broadleaf forest or in a mountain meadow are natural to those habitats, in a city habitat there may be a mixture of native plants and plants introduced by the human inhabitants of the city.

There will also be foods made from plants grown elsewhere and shipped in for the people living in the city to eat. If the other city dwellers, such as mice, find these foods they will happily eat them too!

Primary producers

Plants are called primary producers because they make, or produce, their own food. They are called primary because they are first in the food chain. They capture energy from sunlight and make it available to other living things. Plants are the start of almost every food chain since only plants can provide their own energy from captured sunlight.

Trees and plants in city parks are at the beginning of many urban food chains.

Fantastic photosynthesis

Plants use the energy of sunlight to join up two simple chemicals – carbon dioxide from the air and water from the soil. From these two ingredients the plant makes glucose, a type of sugar. Along with minerals, usually taken from the soil, the plants use this to make new plant material.

Food for all

Plants in towns and cities attract plant-eaters just as plants do in the wilderness. From tiny aphids sucking sap to squirrels cracking nuts and even deer that forage in gardens, animals gather to feast on the plants growing around us.

Some plants produced in the city are not passed on down a food chain. There aren't any grazing animals to eat the grass in parks and gardens, for example, which is why we need lawn mowers!

Rose bushes in city gardens are a good source of food for aphids.

Linking together

Next along the food chain come the animals. They cannot make their own food and so have to eat, or consume, the food that is produced by plants, or they eat other animals that have eaten plants. For this reason animals are called consumers.

Humans contribute to many city food chains by setting up birdfeeders.

Primary consumers

The first animals in the chain are the plant-eaters, also known as herbivores, or primary consumers. The birds coming to the garden birdfeeder are primary consumers, for example, even if they are being fed the type of food they would never get the chance to eat in the wild.

Secondary consumers

Animals that eat other animals are called secondary consumers, or carnivores. In towns and cities carnivores may include raccoons and foxes. Birds of prey, such as kestrels and sparrowhawks, are also attracted to towns and cities where they can catch pigeons and other birds.

Important link

Plant-eaters are perhaps the most important link in the food chain. They are the means by which the energy captured by plants is passed on to the rest of the living world. If the plant-eaters suddenly disappeared then the carnivores would soon follow as they could not switch to eating plants instead.

Omnivores

Animals that eat a wide variety of foods, including plant material and other animals, are called omnivores. These animals are very good at adapting to new habitats and surviving there because their diets are not restricted to only a few things. Successful city omnivores include rats, cockroaches and humans.

Who Eats Who?

bird table

pigeon

peregrine falcon

A peregrine falcon cruises among skyscrapers searching for prey.

Urban food webs

Food chains are a good way of looking at how living things depend on each other for food, but they only tell part of the story. Omnivores, such as rats, don't stay at the same place in the food chain all the time because they can eat both plants and animals.

Because plants are eaten by many different animals, and animals eat and are eaten by a variety of other animals, they can appear in more than one food chain. All the different food chains in a habitat are woven together to form a food web. The food web shows the feeding relationships between plants and animals across a whole habitat.

The rubbish left over from city markets can be a rich source of food for rats and mice.

Yummy!

City rats are real omnivores. They will eat grains, sugar, processed foods, fresh or even rotting fruit and vegetables, insects, birds' eggs, wood, bark and rotten meat and fish raided from our rubbish bins.

Pyramid building

At every link in the chain some energy is lost. Plants need to use some of the energy they capture from the sun as fuel for their own living processes. This means that only some of the captured energy is available to be passed on down the chain. It takes a lot of plants to provide enough energy to support the plant-eaters. Plant-eaters also use up some of the energy they get from the plants for themselves, so they in turn support fewer meat-eaters. This energy relationship can be shown in the form of a food pyramid, with lots of plants or rubbish scraps giving support at the bottom and the plant-eaters and meat-eaters above. Remember this pyramid when you are thinking about feeding relationships between living things in a city.

foxes

mice and rats

plants and rubbish scraps

World-wide web

Human beings bring food to their cities from all over the world. This means that cities are truly part of a world-wide food web, linked together by food chains that stretch around the globe. The plant material that finds its way into a town or city food chain may actually have been grown many kilometres away. For example, peanuts grown in the United States might be hung up in a birdfeeder in a garden in the UK. A compost bin in that same garden might also have apple cores from New Zealand, bean trimmings from Kenya and coffee grounds from Brazil, all decomposing together.

City scavengers

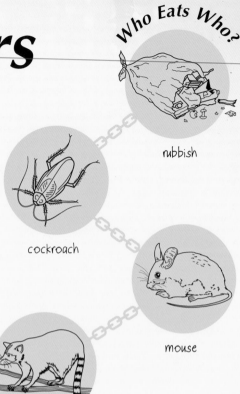

rubbish

cockroach

mouse

raccoon

Putting out plastic bags full of household rubbish for collection is something we all do every week. Sometimes, when we have to clear up afterwards, we find that we've started off another food chain.

A plastic bag will not get in the way of a fox, cat or crow in search of a snack. In North America coyotes and raccoons will also venture into night-time city streets to rummage in the rubbish. In Australia wild dogs, called dingoes, can be a problem.

A raccoon raids a waste bin for food.

Cunning coyotes, rascally raccoons

The coyote is a highly adaptable animal, able to survive in a variety of habitats, including towns and cities. They are good at catching the many rats and mice that share our urban environment and will also pick over discarded rubbish. But they have also been known to attack cats and this will affect the food chain in another way. Some cats eat birds, so where the coyotes kill the cats, there are more birds.

Raccoons are easily identified by the black mask-like markings on their faces and their bushy black and cream banded tails. They are real omnivores and will feed on just about anything. A typical wild raccoon's diet includes fruit and vegetables, insects, birds and their eggs, lizards and small mammals. Raccoons have adapted to life in towns and cities by learning how to open carefully sealed rubbish containers to get at the scraps of food inside.

Who Eats Who?

plant material

pet guinea pig

dingo

Daring dingoes

Pack-hunting dingoes are attracted by the plentiful supply of food on offer in the streets of Australian towns and suburbs. They will eat just about anything, including other wild animals such as bandicoots and wallabies, pet rabbits, guinea pigs and cats, domestic rubbish, leftover pet food and even the contents of the compost heap. Dingoes can be serious pests in farming communities, as they attack livestock. They have no natural enemies.

Dingo

Backyard browsers

City gardeners often seem to find themselves waging war against an army of pests that want to eat their carefully grown plants. Of course, they shouldn't be surprised at this. If you start off a food chain it's only natural that others will join it!

Two frogs in a garden devour a meal of worms.

Pest control

Slugs and snails thrive in gardens where they do considerable damage to big-leafed plants like the gardener's lettuce and cabbages. However, help is at hand because there are actually some animals that like to eat slugs and snails. Among them are frogs, snakes, hedgehogs and birds, such as thrushes. Frogs, in particular, can eat a large number of slugs and snails, although they also find the garden-friendly worms delicious as well. Unfortunately for the frogs, they are often not the last link in the food chain. Snakes, cats, owls, foxes and hedgehogs will all eat frogs.

Downtown deer

People living near woodlands sometimes find that their plants have been munched by something a little larger than a snail. Cities have expanded in many areas and have pushed out into what was once deer territory. The adaptable deer manage to stay hidden in the surviving woodland during the day, but at night they are tempted towards gardens by the plants on display. Bulbs, flowers, shrubs and vegetables, even the bark from trees, can all be stripped away by hungry deer. They are not put off by thorns so even rose bushes provide them with a delicious snack.

Deer love eating roses and are not put off by thorns.

Good deeds rewarded

Flowering plants have to be pollinated before they can produce seeds. This means that pollen has to be carried from one flower to another, sometimes on the same plant, sometimes on other plants. The pollen carriers in gardens and parks are usually insects, such as bees and butterflies. The flowers 'pay' the insects for this service by providing them with sweet, energy-rich nectar. When the insects visit the flower to feed, pollen sticks to their bodies and is carried with them to the next flower they visit.

Water wildlife

Many towns and cities have water features. These can range from rivers and canals flowing through a town to small ponds in gardens. All of these can prove attractive to wildlife.

Egret

Down by the riverside

Wildlife has been making a remarkable return to many city rivers that were once too polluted to support life. The waterways around New York City, for example, are now home to flocks of water birds, such as herons, egrets and ibises. These birds feed on a wide variety of animals that live in the water, including fish, frogs, reptiles, smaller birds and mammals, insects and shellfish.

The River Thames flowing through London was once heavily polluted. Just fifty years ago there were no fish to be found in the stretch of the Thames that flowed through central London. Now more than a hundred different kinds of fish are found in the river, including salmon, sea bass and flounder.

These fish depend on a wide variety of food sources. Some are herbivores, which nibble water plants. Others may feed on insects and other minibeast plant-eaters. Some fish even eat other fish. The fish living in the river bring fish-eating birds, such as cormorants, to the Thames as well.

A heron stalks a fish in a pond.

Pondlife

Garden ponds are rich mini-habitats. As with all habitats, ponds depend on healthy green plants to provide food for the other living things. Pond plants can range from microscopic algae in the water to large rushes growing around the edge. Water fleas and snails eat the pond plants. Predators such as dragonfly larvae eat the herbivores. A large pond might even attract water voles and birds such as herons, ducks and kingfishers.

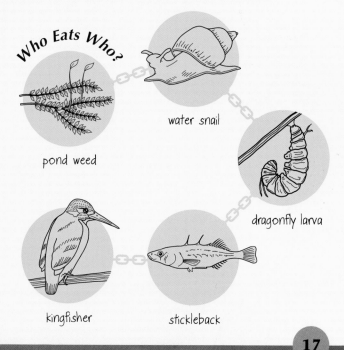

Who Eats Who?

pond weed

water snail

dragonfly larva

kingfisher

stickleback

Flying visits

Birds, with their ability to fly, are well adapted to paying a visit to city parks and gardens. Towns and cities in Australia play host to noisy and colourful flocks of galahs, kookaburras and cockatoos. North American gardeners can see hummingbirds, cardinals and bluejays. In Europe, blackbirds, tits and finches are common garden visitors.

Cockatoos often visit Australian gardens.

Bird feeders

Birds come to parks and gardens in search of food, and sometimes to find places to build their nests too. Birds will eat garden insects, worms and other small creatures. They will also peck at flower buds, fruits and seedheads on garden plants and shrubs.

We're in the chain!

Many types of songbirds are helped through the winter months by generous humans and their birdtables.

Wasps build nests in gardens. They are an essential part of city food chains.

An unexpected chain

People who put out seeds and nuts to attract birds to their gardens are setting up a link in a food chain, because by putting out food for songbirds the gardener may attract other visitors that they don't want.

Birds gathering around food on a birdtable or feeder are going to draw the attention of bird-eating predators. The birdlover may find that there is a hawk perched in a tree ready to pounce on the songbirds. If the birds make a nest in the garden, crows will be ready to snatch up eggs and chicks. And local cats may soon take an interest in the birdtable, too.

Watch that wasp!

For many people the wasp is nothing but a pest, but this is wrong. Wasps are an essential part of garden food webs. Unlike the nectar-loving bee, the wasp is a carnivore. It hunts down caterpillars and other insects that damage plants, and takes them away in its powerful jaws to feed the grubs back at its nest.

Despite their stings, wasps are not immune from being attacked and eaten themselves. Birds such as starlings and blackbirds will catch and eat wasps. There are also certain spiders that specialise in catching wasps.

Green gardens

Just about any garden or backyard can become an attractive haven for wildlife. It can support many different food chains, which may include insects, birds and frogs as well as occasional predators, such as snakes, that come to eat them. Making a garden compost heap can create an entirely different variety of new food chains.

Urban recycling

City food webs are different from those of the desert or the rainforest because, as we have seen, the city's human inhabitants are constantly renewing the food supply. This means that it is less essential for some urban wildlife that resources are recycled. Of course, this doesn't mean that recycling doesn't happen. And it certainly doesn't mean that we humans shouldn't encourage it.

A wide variety of garden plants attracts visitors such as this garter snake.

Worms thrive on compost heaps.

Keep on composting!

Compost heaps are a wonderful way to recycle household and garden waste products efficiently. A good compost heap will become home to countless minibeasts.

Mixing in soil adds fungi and bacteria to the compost. These multiply rapidly as they work to break down the waste products. Worms, woodlice, ants, beetles and other creatures soon find their way to the rich compost food supply.

The web within

Inside the compost heap a number of food chains soon become established. As with most other food chains, plants are still the primary producers at the start of the chain. They just happen to be dead rather than living plants.

Moulds are primary consumers and grow on the plant remains. They are eaten by mould mites, which are secondary consumers. In turn, predatory centipedes, one of the top consumers in the compost food web, may devour the mites and later be eaten in turn by a mouse.

Who Eats Who?

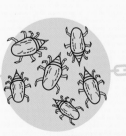

moulds on an orange

mites

centipede

mouse

Unwelcome guests

It's nice to have natural things around our homes. We can all enjoy trees in our parks and gardens and the birds that sing in their branches. However, there are some animals that aren't so welcome, and which sometimes get a little too close for comfort.

Cockroaches

In their original tropical forest habitat cockroaches play a valuable role as nature's recyclers, scavenging on dead plant material. When messy humans leave food around their homes it is perhaps inevitable that cockroaches will move in to 'clean up' there as well.

Cockroaches thrive in the warm, moist environments found in kitchens, hiding beneath fridges and under sinks. They also live in sewers and will often get into homes that way.

There are few cockroach-eaters that can follow the cockroach into our homes. One is a type of wasp that lays its eggs in the cockroach's eggcases. The emerging young wasp then feeds on the unhatched cockroach.

Yummy!

Mice and rats like to eat everything we like, and even some things we don't, such as soap and tobacco!

A hungry cockroach feeds on a fruit bowl.

A fox hunts mice in a garden.

Rats and mice

Rats and mice are among the most successful of the animals to have joined us in our towns and cities. They often make their nests in and around buildings such as warehouses and people's homes. Both are omnivores and cause a lot of damage to food stocks as well as gnawing wood and other materials.

Travelling the world

The house mouse originally came from southern Asia and has spread around the world by hitching a ride with human travellers. Norway rats, one of the most common urban species, actually originated in China and spread in the same way as mice.

Cats and foxes

Inside the home mice and rats are safe from predators, apart from the household cat, if there is one. If they venture outside they may be at risk of being eaten by another city visitor, the fox. A fox on a mousehunt will keep very still as it listens and watches as an unsuspecting mouse draws near. Then it will leap up suddenly, bringing its forepaws down to pin the mouse to the ground.

We're in the chain!

About half of an urban fox's diet may come from human handouts. Lots of people like to encourage foxes by leaving out food scraps.

Killer cats?

The top predator in many urban food chains might just be curled up close to you right now. Don't be fooled; the peaceful pussycat purring nearby is an accomplished hunter.

Even well-fed pet cats such as this one will hunt when outside.

Following instinct

By one estimate, pet and farm cats in the UK alone could be killing as many as 275 million items of prey, including 55 million birds, every year. The most common small mammals caught by cats are mice and voles. The blue wren, once a common bird in Australia, is now rare in areas where domestic cats roam.

European import

The domestic cat was taken to North America and Australia by European settlers a few hundred years ago. Since then their numbers have grown. Today there may be 100 million or more cats in the USA, for example, many of them living in the wild.

Cats are highly skilled hunters and even the mildest pet has the potential to play its part in nature's food chain as a killer of prey when it slips out through the catflap. This instinct is very strong in cats and no matter how well fed they are at home, some cats still kill, even though they don't always eat what they catch.

Balance of nature

Every year many millions of animals die naturally of disease and starvation. Cats, like other predators, tend to catch weak and sickly animals. This means that at least some of the birds and other animals killed by cats would have died from other causes anyway.

According to the UK's Royal Society for the Protection of Birds there is no scientific evidence to prove that cats have any real impact on declining bird populations. Nevertheless, cats are without doubt major predators of wildlife.

Who Eats Who?

insect   bird   cat

Cats kill up to 55 million birds in Britain every year.

Wasteland wildlife

Cities are very good at producing waste. Tonnes of rubbish are removed from cities every day, often to landfill sites. These gigantic rubbish heaps can become thriving wildlife habitats.

Living in the landfill

Landfill sites contain a large amount of food material and this attracts insects such as wasps and flies, which come to feed on the rubbish and lay their eggs on the decaying material. Bacteria flourish in the tip and they create warmth as they break down the food wastes. This warmth creates the right conditions for cockroaches and other beetles to survive. They too find plenty to eat amongst the rubbish.

In turn, mice and other small mammals are attracted to the warmth and ready supply of food. Larger animals such as foxes and bears will come to forage for food and to catch the mice. In many parts of Europe white storks can be seen striding over waste tips in search of a tasty morsel to eat.

A North American black bear raids a rubbish bag.

Seagull city

Flocks of seagulls will fly many kilometres inland from their usual seashore habitat to pick over the scraps available on a landfill site. They come especially in the winter months when natural food sources might be harder to find. In Australia, one seagull colony increased from just a few pairs to over 50,000 pairs in fifty years as a result of the birds making use of landfill food.

Bear necessities

In parts of North America bears visit rubbish tips. Bears adapt easily to living near towns and cities and won't hesitate to raid a tip in search of food. Bears can soon learn to look for human food in other places and will visit garden compost heaps and household rubbish containers.

Some bolder bears will even enter kitchens or supermarkets in search of food. Very rarely bears will attack, injure or even kill people who disturb them. Sadly, because of this risk, many 'nuisance' bears end up being shot every year.

A flock of seagulls fights over domestic rubbish on a tip.

City food web

Here is a city habitats food web. Surrounding it are some fascinating city habitat facts.

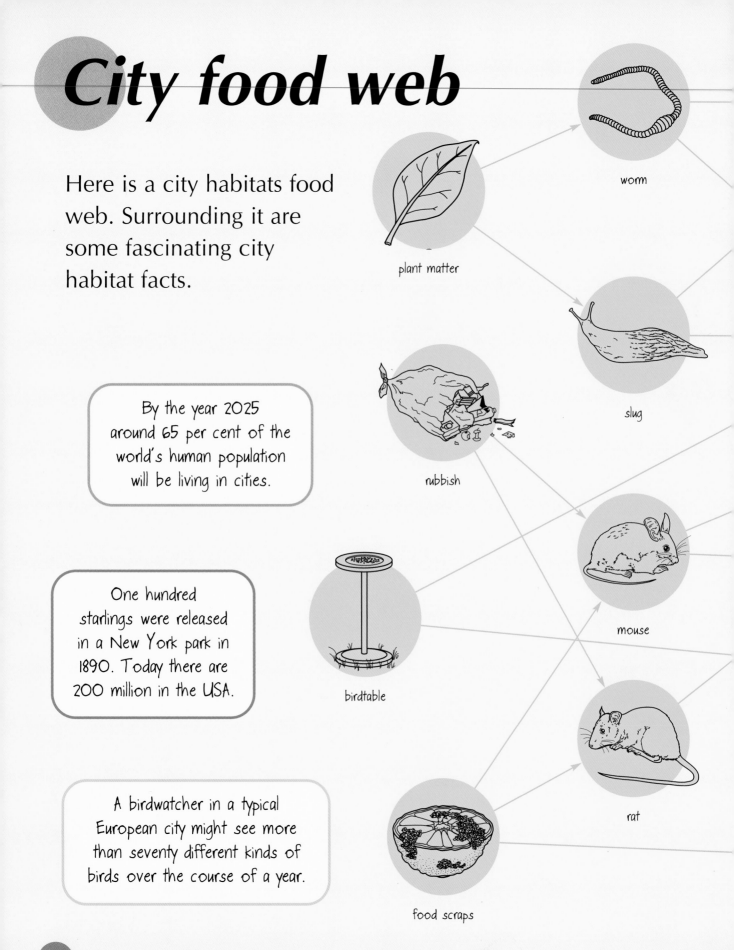

plant matter

worm

slug

rubbish

birdtable

mouse

rat

food scraps

By the year 2025 around 65 per cent of the world's human population will be living in cities.

One hundred starlings were released in a New York park in 1890. Today there are 200 million in the USA.

A birdwatcher in a typical European city might see more than seventy different kinds of birds over the course of a year.

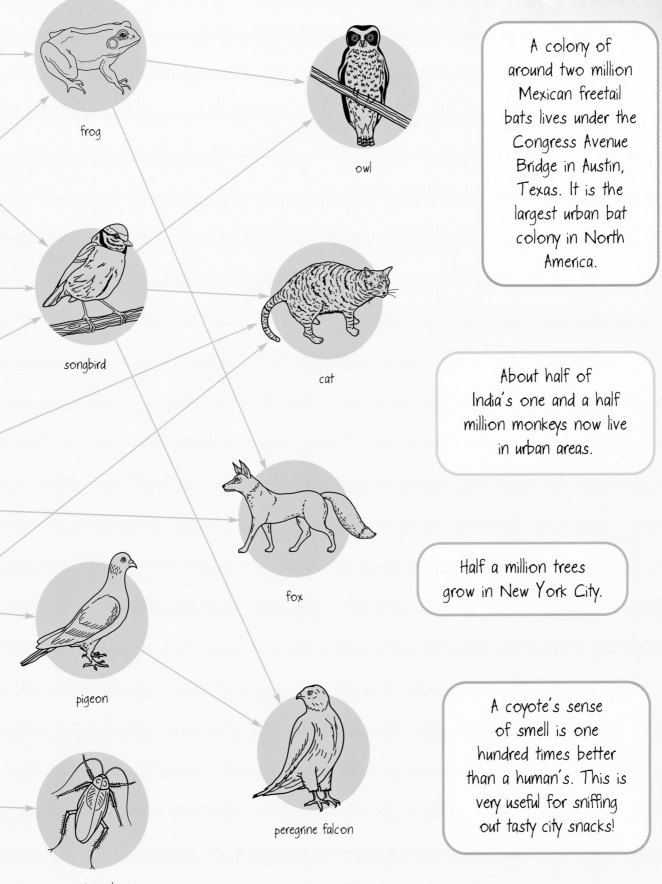

frog

owl

songbird

cat

fox

pigeon

peregrine falcon

cockroach

A colony of around two million Mexican freetail bats lives under the Congress Avenue Bridge in Austin, Texas. It is the largest urban bat colony in North America.

About half of India's one and a half million monkeys now live in urban areas.

Half a million trees grow in New York City.

A coyote's sense of smell is one hundred times better than a human's. This is very useful for sniffing out tasty city snacks!

Glossary

adapted

suited to life in a particular environment.

algae

microscopic plants that are usually found growing in water.

aphid

a tiny plant-eating insect, also known as the greenfly, which can seriously damage crops.

bacteria

microscopic organisms that are found just about everywhere. They are very important decomposers.

carnivore

a meat-eating animal.

consumer

an organism that eats another living thing to get energy; primary consumers eat plants, secondary consumers eat animals.

decomposer

a living thing that feeds on and breaks down dead plants and animals as well as animal waste.

diversity

the range of things found in a certain place.

environment

a physical habitat such as a rainforest, desert or a city, together with all the living things that make their home there.

grub

a young insect that has not grown legs yet.

habitat

the place where a living thing has a home.

herbivore

an animal that eats plants.

immune

able to resist being harmed by something.

micro-organism

a living thing that is so small it can only be seen under a microscope.

native

an animal or plant that is found naturally in a particular place.

nectar

a sweet, energy-rich liquid produced by flowers to attract pollinating animals such as bees.

organism

a living thing.

omnivore

an animal that eats a broad range of things, including various plant materials and other animals. Omnivores such as rats, mice, cockroaches and humans are highly successful city dwellers.

photosynthesis

the process by which plants capture the energy of sunlight and use it to make sugar.

pollination

the process by which grains of pollen are carried from one flower to another, usually by bees; when pollination has taken place seeds can begin to form.

predator

an animal that kills and eats other animals.

producer

an organism that makes, or produces, its own food; producers are the source of energy for the rest of the food chain.

scavenger

an animal that eats dead or dying things including leftovers from another animal's meal. Urban foxes and coyotes will scavenge in rubbish bins, for example.

recycling

re-using waste materials.

urban

relating to towns and cities.

Towns and City Websites

http://www.urbanneighbors.nypl.org

Discover the wild side of New York City.

http://www.bbc.co.uk/nature/animals/wildbritain/wildinyourgarden/gardens/

A guide to garden wildlife, including virtual wildlife gardens.

http://www.gunnar.cc/cgi-bin/ringlink/list.pl?ringid=urbanwildlife;siteid=fbcp

A list of sites dedicated to urban wildlife around the world.

http://www.bc-alter.net/critter/OurWorld.htm

A site dedicated to looking after Canadian urban wildlife.

Index